Or my parents
Miguel and Concepción
GS

Catalogue and e-commerce
Our catalogue of books and other products can be consulted on:
http://www.msm-editions.fr
http://www.msm-publishers.com
These are business sites with secure on-line payment.

BP 20, 65502 Vic-en-Bigorre Cedex - France

Dépôt légal : February 2004
ISBN 978-2-9078-9964-2

Printed by Llob 3, Barberà del Vallès – Spain (June 2010)

Noune

Child of Prehistory

Drawings : Gemma Sales
Text : Michel Vaidis

Scientific Adviser,
Prehistory Laboratory, Musée de l'Homme

A long, long time ago, only animals lived on the Earth... One day, one of them stood up on his back legs and started to walk... And so the first humans appeared... They lived just outside huge caves and ate raw flesh which they managed to steal off other animals.

Little by little these humans became cleverer with their hands. They saw that by breaking stones they could get splinters with sharp cutting edges. This was useful for cutting up meat. It was handy, too, for scraping and cutting the skins that they used for clothes. Then they began to work stone to make tools and weapons.

This is how these humans lived for hundreds of thousands of years... They discovered fire which gave them warmth and light, and protected them from wild beasts. With fire they roasted meat and boiled water. They learnt how to make fire, and then how to keep fires alight.

Thousands and thousands of years went by. Humans made new discoveries which made their lives less difficult. The way they looked changed, too. And they ended up looking pretty much the way we look today.

Some seventeen thousand years ago, a group of men and women pitched their camp beneath a huge overhanging crag. From the top you could look down on a beautiful valley with a gently meandering river.

Their tents were made of reindeer skins. They looked like the tents which American Indians used much later on.

The chief of these people was called Pah. His son, Noune, had a big sister called Malina. She helped her mother, Mah, with day-to-day tasks. Of all the little boys in the camp, Noune was the most inquisitive. He would not let a moment go by without asking a question:
"Why are you doing that?"–"What's that?"–"What's that for?"

Noune liked watching his sister light the fire. She would make a little pile of dry moss, and bury a bit of soft wood in it. Then she would place the tip of a wooden stick on the soft wood and turn the stick very fast between her hands. In no time a wisp of smoke would appear. That was when Noune blew on it and the whole thing, moss and all, burst into flames.

It was Mah's job to get meals ready.
"Why do you put stones in the fire?" Noune asked his mother, who replied: "When they're burning hot, I'll put them in the water to make it boil. Then I'll put pieces of meat into the water, with some herbs and roots, and when it's all cooked, we'll eat it."

"They're back! They're back!"
The men were returning from the hunt. Noune ran off to meet them.
"Let me take your spears, Pah!"
Noune puffed out his chest, proud to be carrying his father's weapons, and the hunters said:
"Look how strong he is. It's Noune the hunter!"

In those days many reindeer lived in the valley. The reindeer was of great value for humans. They ate its flesh, and made clothes with its skin. They used its antlers to make weapons and tools. And they carved fine needles from its bones. Every part of the reindeer was used. This is why Pah was always telling Noune to treat this handsome creature with respect, because it gave them so many things.

"Ow!"
While Malina's back was turned, Noune had grabbed the needle she was using to sew a skin.
"Serves you right! You shouldn't meddle... Anyway, this is a girl's job! You're not a girl are you?"
Noune sucked the little drop of blood at the tip of his finger. He was a bit upset, so he went off to find Mougo.

"What are you doing?" he asked.
"I'm carving a spear-thrower," the man replied.
The little boy watched Mougo's sharp chisel etch a pretty little horse.
"Why a horse?" Noune asked.
"So that the spear will be as swift as a galloping horse."
Then Noune picked up two bits of wood lying nearby and pretended to throw a spear.

"Please take me to see the reindeer at the ford across the river...", Noune asked Pah.
The water was shallow at the ford. This is where horses and reindeer came to drink and cross the river. Noune and Pah hid in the tall grass and watched the reindeer quenching their thirst.

All of a sudden, Noune spied a lynx creeping up on a fawn that had strayed from its mother.
"He's going to kill it... stop him!", Noune whispered. Pah took his sling and hurled a spear. It hit the lynx just as it was about to leap on the fawn.

Malina made a bag with the lynx's skin and used it for gathering food. The teeth were given to Mougo, so he could put holes through them and make a pretty necklace for Noune.

Pah used their little adventure to explain to Noune that there was danger everywhere. He told him never to leave the camp on his own: a small boy was no match for a ravenous lynx. The strongest would always win.

When autumn came the willows and elms turned beautiful colours. The wind grew colder and sent the leaves whirling around.

Noune watched a squirrel gathering acorns and hiding them in a hole in an old oak tree. Malina appeared carrying her new bag.
"Where are you going?" Noune asked.
"Come with me. I'll show you," she replied.

"Why are you collecting those little brown pebbles?" Noune asked.
"They're hazelnuts. They're good to eat," she answered.
He picked one up and put it in his mouth.
"Ow! It's hard!"
Then his sister showed him how to crack open the shell with a stone.

All the women made the most of the last fine days to gather medicinal herbs, dig up the last edible roots, and pick the last berries before winter would cover the valley in a thick mantle of snow.

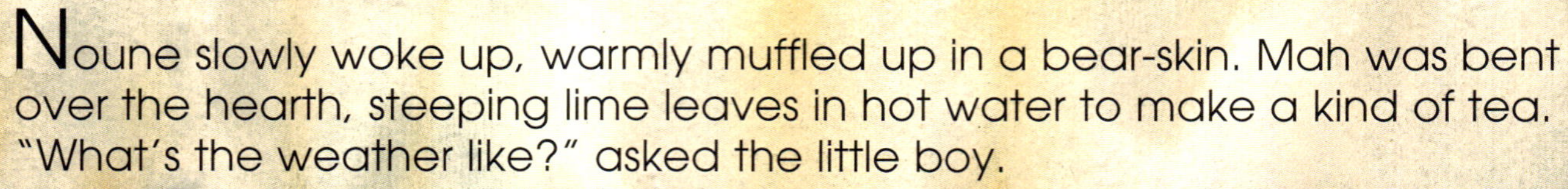

Noune slowly woke up, warmly muffled up in a bear-skin. Mah was bent over the hearth, steeping lime leaves in hot water to make a kind of tea.
"What's the weather like?" asked the little boy.
"Take a look for yourself", Malina said.
Noune got up and poked his head outside the tent.
"Oh!" he cried out in surprise. Snow had fallen during the night.

Malina was knotting badger hairs on to a small stick.
"What's that for?" asked Noune, puzzled.
"It's for spreading on the colour. The whole clan's going to meet in the great cave to paint the animals that we'll see again next spring."

It was very dark in the great cave. Flares sent large shadows dancing across the walls.
Noune felt nervous, despite the stone oil-lamp which gave off a warm glow. Its small flame flickered at the end of a woven wick soaked in reindeer fat. Malina told him how it was the burning fat that kept the flame alight.

Pah and Mougo had climbed up some scaffolding made of pine wood. They were so high up that they could touch the roof of the cave. With a stub of charcoal, Pah drew the outline of an animal. Noune recognized it and called out:
"It's a bull. Pah's drawn a bull!"

Mah was pounding ochre-coloured earth. She mixed it with the reindeer fat to make the colours which Mougo then spread on the rock with the brush Malina had made.

Winter was nearly over. In the great cave, Pah and Mougo had decorated most of the roof and the whole of one wall.

Noune was amazed. It was so beautiful. It looked so like what he had seen in the valley, he had the impression that the horses and bulls and deer he saw before him were about to leap off the walls and dash out of the cave.

"Which animal is the meanest?" asked the little boy.
"No animals are mean. They have to kill to feed themselves, and they have to run away to keep from being eaten themselves. That's the way life is," his father replied.

Then Pah told Noune how bison stampeded, raising clouds of dust, how brown bears stood up on their hind legs to steal honey from bees' nests, how wolves surrounded reindeer to hunt them better, and how ibex could clamber up slopes so steep that people could never keep their balance on them.

"And which is the biggest animal?" Noune went on.
"The mammoth, but he lives far away in the vast steppes in the north."
Noune daydreamed for a moment about those huge beasts and asked yet another question.
"And the most cunning?"
Pah burst out laughing.
"Humans."
"But... we don't have claws or fangs...", Noune said.
"Yes, but we know how to make the tools and weapons we need. We've got fire. And we think before we do things."

Noune had gone fishing with Mougo. For a long time he watched Mougo standing stockstill looking deep into the water. Suddenly a kingfisher dived into the river and emerged with a brightly-coloured little fish in its beak.
"Look! He can catch fish!" exclaimed Noune.
"Me too...", said Mougo, throwing his harpoon.
"And this one's much bigger," he said, pulling out an enormous salmon flapping on the tip of the harpoon.

Next day Noune pretended he was Mougo the fisherman. Balanced on a large stone jutting above the water of a small stream, he called out to his sister who was having a swim.
"Watch me catch a salmon!"
Carried away by his own excitement, Noune toppled into the water. Malina burst out laughing.
"And I'll show you how to fish for little boys!"

The reindeer had left the valley and gone to their summer grazing grounds. The people had packed up their camp beneath the crag and followed them.
"Why are we leaving?", Noune sobbed.
"We'll come back in the autumn with the reindeer," Mah promised.

They met some people from another camp and exchanged clothes and tools. One of the men showed Noune a small bird's bone. It was hollow and had several holes in it.

"What's it for?" the little boy asked straightaway, still as inquisitive as ever.

"Blow into it and cover the little holes with your fingers, one by one."

First, Noune blew too hard and nothing happened. He tried again, not so hard this time. A very low whistle came from the bone.

Everyone clapped and the man gave Noune the little flute as a present.

Noune grew up and became a famous hunter. So did his children, and their children too. Then the centuries passed and everyone forgot about those humans... until one day when four children were exploring an underground passage, and quite by chance they came upon the great cave of Noune.